Grief comes in many forms, but it's never in disguise. In Roseanne Freed's *Your Name Is a Poem*, grief takes the form of sadness, loss, and overwhelming love, seen through a mother's eyes. From her young daughter's response to an unexpected Christmas gift ("Are you going to take it away?") to the pain of angry answers to "How are you doing?", there is an unbroken thread of a mother's love that never falters. That love—overlayed with the sadness of not being able to stop her daughter's cancer, not being allowed to share the difficult journey, not being allowed to say that last goodbye—love is the ultimate urn that keeps her grief contained, but never forgotten. *Your Name Is a Poem* is honest and personal, letting the reader see and share the sorrow of losing a child whose name means "tenderness."

—j. lewis, editor of *Verse-Virtual* and author of *goodbye sounds like* pictureshowpress.net

Cover Image Credit: Roseanne Freed
Author Image Credit: Angus MacNeil

FIRST EDITION

ISBN-13: 979-8-9850690-5-1

your name is a poem

Roseanne Freed

Picture Show Press

In loving memory of my daughter Mahalia Nandi Freed
(July 17, 1978 – February 23, 2020)

May her memory be for a blessing.

"Poetry gives the griever not release from grief, but companionship in grief."

—Donald Hall

POEMS

Your Name Is a Poem

Before you were born,
I knew you were someone special
and needed a unique name;
there are too many girls called
Jennifer, Jessica, or Jane.

After a long search
—not easy in the days before Google—
I found your name in a library book.
Though we didn't know the sex
of our unborn child
we didn't choose a boy's name
because once we saw Mahalia,
and learned it means
"tenderness" in Hebrew,
we knew you were our Mahalia.

And like Oprah, Cher and Madonna
you have always been known
by your first name.

Sleepless

I knew you'd cry once my head kissed
the pillow, but praying for a few minutes
of rest I lay down anyway,

my nighty damp with milk and sweat,
every one of those sleep-deprived
summer nights after your birth.

Only your insistent wailing
and my maternal instinct dragged me
from my bed. A single glance

at you, my sweet-smelling, mewling
miracle, your little head wet
with humidity, your arms

and legs calling for me—
I'd forget my weariness
or that I stank of a dairy.

With the world in my arms,
a love I've never known
filled my heart, and milk

spouted like a fountain,
spraying you—your face,
your hair, even up your nose.

As you gulped my liquid love,
your little hand grasped my finger,
and you gave a crooked smile.

How Did He Know?

Mahalia knew Canadian children
slept in fleecy, one-piece jammies

with attached feet because of the snow
and cold in the winter.

Age three and a half she saw a girl
on TV in a nightgown, and asked for one.

Children who don't stay under the covers,
don't wear nighties, I said,

I promise to stay under my blankie,
she said,

I don't want you to get sick.
Maybe when you go to big school.

Several months later on Christmas day—
her first present from Santa,

a pink-and-white striped nightgown.
Size four.

How did he know I wanted a nightie?
How did the reindeer know my house?

Are you going to take it away?
she whispered, tears filling her eyes.

I'll never take away a gift from Santa.
It's yours to keep.

That's all she needed
to believe in herself.

Our Time Together, Too Short

My sweet Mahalia, born after two days labor
with all those lucky sevens—
17/7/78 at 7:07 pm weighing 7 lbs. 7 oz.,

the baby who grew fat and healthy
nursing at my breast for a whole year,
the one-year-old

who crawled into the fridge
to get at the pickles and olives,
but didn't care for cake, or candy,

the little cutie (she was always small)
with an infectious laugh, who loved
the hot sun and running around in the nude,

the inquisitive, intelligent child
with a remarkable early command of language,
who'd put a book in my hand, climb

onto my lap, and wait for me to read,
her favorite stories from age two
were of the two Peters—Rabbit and Pan—

the munchkin who hung upside down
from the top of the jungle gym
her dad built under the cherry tree,

the toothless Tinker Bell
with a bag of Halloween
candy she forgot to eat,

the girl who rode bikes and horses,
hiked, swam, and canoed
in Northern lakes every summer,

the young woman passionate about healing
and herbs, who became a Naturopathic Doctor,
birthed her two children at home,

but never cared about cars, preferring
to ride her bike—even to chemo
dates in the Canadian winter.

I loved her even when I didn't love her.

Big Sister I

1982

Mahalia begged for a baby sister.
When her brother was born
she was disappointed,
but didn't take long to forgive him.

Four years older than her brother,
she was the best big sister.

When we brought our new baby home,
she slept on the floor
in our room, under his crib,
refused to go back to her bed
until we moved him
into her room.

The first time she held him
he threw up on her.
She cried, then kissed him,
He's just a baby.

Big Sister II

2003

One bitterly cold Sunday
in January
—Mahalia in medical school in Toronto,
Jeremy in 2nd year university near Montreal,
their father and I in Los Angeles—
our son's building caught fire.

Everyone escaped,
some in their pajamas,
most without coats.
Our clever boy grabbed
yesterday's clothes
off the floor—
the worst pair of pants
he owned, held on
at the waist with safety pins.

The thirty-eight students
lost everything.

He phoned from the campus,
woke us up with: *I'm OK.*
Our building burned down. All I own in the world
is a pair of ragged jeans and a winter jacket.
I've got library books and photo albums in my room,
and beer and pizza in the fridge.
I have no bed, no books, no computer, no home,
he cried. And I cried with him.

Why did we move so far
from our children?

Ten minutes later a call
from big sister:
no need for us parents
to fly from California.
Easier for her to go to Quebec.
She'd ask her prof
if she could miss an exam.

Grateful and relieved
to be spared the trip,
I've carried the guilt ever since.

Wrong Question

My son phones from the hospital
giving me a chance to speak to his sister
fighting for her life—
her fourth surgery in eighteen months.

I'm unsure what to say,
she's always critical of me,
ignores my texts
or says, *Wrong question.*

Last time I asked *How are you?*
she replied,

> *I have impacted two-year-old fecal matter,*
> *constant rectal spasms*
> *and a healing abdominal incision.*
> *Not a great combo, or a question I can answer.*

Don't ask silly questions
I tell myself,
and jabber like an idiot
about showers and stickers for her kids,
never realizing this is going to be
the second to last time

I ever speak to her.

A Fearful Thing

'Tis a fearful thing to love what death can touch.
—Rabbi Chaim Stern

Soup, I thought, after the colonoscopy
when they said your colon
was blocked by a tumor.

A pot of my lentil soup,
our staple meal through the Canadian
winters of your childhood.

In the hospital, after the devastating
diagnosis of stage four cancer,
the doctors didn't use the word *cure*—

you did. Before the first of your four
surgeries, and the bi-weekly
chemo appointments, you said:

> *I'm an ND. I know what to do,*
> *what herbs to take along with the chemo.*
> *I'll be a miracle written up in books.*

But tumors don't care about miracles,
or forty-year-old Naturopaths
with two children under five.

After fifteen months of treatments
the oncologist looked at your PET scan:
The chemo didn't work. Sorry.

That night you told me you'd always
hated my soup. Though your words
stung, I didn't comment, didn't need

the last word. Because I love you,
I understood your pain and frustration,
and knew you wouldn't give up and go home

to die. You increased your daily supplements,
gave yourself mistletoe injections, had acupuncture,
and something called nebulized DCA treatments.

Two months later you wrote on Facebook:

> *In pain twenty-four/seven, barely able to stand.*
> *If anyone tells me I'm strong*
> *I might show my strength by punching them.*

Aching to connect with you, Dad and I chose
comfort in the pottery bowls you made
when you were ten. We hadn't used them

in years. I sent you a text:
We're eating soup in your bowls.
Mine has pink hearts.

You replied. Immediately.

> *I miss eating.*

That was your last message to me.
You died the next day.

This Isn't About You

Your daughter is dying. You don't understand
why she doesn't want you at her bedside,
and write to her friend Jane, *I fear*
I'll always regret obeying her wish not to come.

Jane replies,

> *Mahalia sees your photos*
> *every time she opens her eyes.*

Does she think that comforts you?

You say,

I've spoken with her once.
Can I speak to her again?

Jane responds,

> *You're the only person she's called.*
> *Take that gift.*

That five-minute conversation, a gift?
Obeying the instructions, you didn't mention
cancer, or her imminent death,
before fluid filled her lungs,
and the nurse ended the call.

When updates come—

via texts from Jane,

> *She stood briefly today.*
> *Still refuses visitors.*

or your daughter's Facebook page,

Tumors visibly growing
Many scans. Many meds. So much pain.

or when Jane writes,

Her time is close. She sleeps most of the time.

you ache knowing you should be there.

When you text:

I don't understand her wish to exclude me.

Jane, mother of two says,

This isn't about you.

You don't bother to reply.

Unstoppable

The cancer is everywhere.
I'm so very sorry, the doctor said.

    How will I die? my daughter asked.

I don't know which organs
will shut down first,
possibly liver failure
or drowning in fluid from your lungs.

The two children were told:
    Mama's cancer is serious,
    the doctors can't help her.
    She's going to die and won't come back.

The children came separately to say goodbye.

Isaiah, age two, asked about the tube in her nose,
tried hard not to jump on the bed,
wanted to put everything in his mouth—
even masks and gloves on the floor by the trash.

Ellemere, age four, colored a picture
with Mama in the Mandala book,
and sobbed in her room after the visit.

Mahalia chose to die with her family.
Ellemere held her hand. Isaiah sat in her lap.

Ready? the doctor asked.
Can one be ready when only 41?

    Remember, Mama isn't going to sleep.
    She will be dead.

Before taking her last breath
her final words to her children—
Do you know how much I love you?

A few minutes after she passed
Isaiah said, *When will she wake up?*

Six months later he said,
I want to see Mama.

Twelve months later he told me,
Mama isn't coming back. She died.

The Stranger

At my mother's funeral the rabbi asked,
Who wants to see the body before we close the coffin?
It was good to see her. Wrapped

in a white cloth, she looked peaceful,
like the nun she'd always wanted to be.
I even kissed her cold forehead.

To help us accept our daughter had died
I knew her father and I had to see her,
had to see the body.

We didn't recognize the person
in the coffin, arms folded across her chest
at our private viewing. Pain

deeply etched on this stranger's
face, her cheeks fevered, and her belly
—oh god her belly—inflated

from the total bowel blockage
looked nine months pregnant.
I hoped my husband didn't notice.

We stared silently, suffocated
by the truth
of how much she'd suffered.

I touched her hand,
and kissed her cold forehead.
It didn't comfort.

I don't know how people take pictures
or cut off locks of hair
from their beloveds' bodies.

I lit the candles on the table,
held my spouse's hand,
and we both wept.

A Week After She Left Us My Therapist Told Me

You no longer need to hold back your emotions.
You have full permission to feel your feelings.
It's healthy and important.

I can't.
If I allow myself to weep
I hear her—

    Stop making it about you.

"A Poem Begins With a Lump in the Throat"

after Robert Frost

Sunday will be six weeks
since our daughter died.

My mouth eats without hunger.
My pillow forgets how to sleep.
Mail piles up on the table—
six issues of *The New Yorker*
unopened.

People of the Lakota tribe believe
a grieving person is holy,
closer to the spirit world,
inhaling a natural wisdom
with our sorrow.

I don't feel holy,
or wise.

I put her pictures all over the house.
Her father calls them ghosts.

Signs

Your daughter is going to send you butterflies,
a psychic told me last month.
I see them.
You can't not see a butterfly if it follows
you along an empty trail.
Hello, I say, *Thank you for coming,*
and blow kisses.

The pandemic forces us to honor
her memory remotely.
Using our computers, we join Shabbat services
from her synagogue in Vancouver.

Today's service opens with three women singing
a cappella in the shul garden,
and when it continues with the mourner's
kaddish, the two-thousand-year-old prayer
for the souls of our departed
loved ones that begins,
Yitgadal v'yitkadash sh'mei raba,
a cabbage white flies in circles above their heads.

Shabbat Shalom, Mahalia.

The Hardest Part

Your life will never be the same,
Suzanne said after my daughter passed away.

The hardest part?
The rawness of grief.
The nightmare doesn't end with the rising sun.
No cups of tea can cure
the inconsolable ache or fatigue.

Though her death wasn't sudden
it wasn't expected.

After the diagnosis her message to us,
Don't weep or be depressed
I am determined to fight this.
And win.

I believed her.
We all did.
Don't you have to be old to die?

I prayed.
Yes, the atheist prayed.

When the oncologist said,
Only a few weeks,
she hid her fear of dying.
In constant pain, she took opioids
so she could hug her small children.

I altered my prayers, offered
to shave my hair,
forgo meat, alcohol, chocolates.

She died.

The hardest part?
Learning to say—
May her memory be for a blessing
about my child.

Nine Months

Nine months since you left us, in my grief
I surrender to junk food and an evening
glass of wine with chips.

>   Such excitement to watch you grow
>   inside me, to feel you moving about
>   first as little flutters like a mouse,

I know the wine is a crutch,
but it's just one glass and I need it.
Like I need coffee in the morning.

>   Later when a hand or foot
>   punched out my belly,
>   Pa and I shared tears of happiness.

I'm thankful for the coronavirus fashion
of pants with elastic waists to hide
the pandemic pounds on my bum and belly.

>   I played classical music
>   to my welcome guest, ate healthy,
>   did yoga, swam twice a week at the Y,

My daily swims in our pool
help my sadness.
You also loved swimming.

>   I discovered unconditional love
>   at your birth, and such nachas
>   as you grew fat from my breast.

Erin gave me your favorite sweater.
Wearing it doesn't comfort me—
it just reminds me how wrong this is.

How Deep in the Valley

While passing the time in a coffee shop
with a latte and Facebook,
a photo pops up of you on a lawn

of dandelions. I laugh to see your elfin face,
short, punky, chestnut hair, silver ring
in your nose. *Salut* Mahalia,

you didn't die! It's been a bad dream.
I look again. I see it's a three-year-old *memory*.
You and Ellemere in the purple sweaters

you knitted. A happy day with your baby
and your favorite weed, before the cancer
took you from us. With cruel

timing, the song we sang at your funeral,
Sarah Harmer's *How Deep in the Valley*,
plays on the sound system. I weep for you,

my firstborn child. Twelve months now.
Friends say *Sorry*. Surprised I'm still grieving.
It comforts. Sometimes. After a parent buries

a child there is no gentle choreography to help
us through to the other side, past grief.
There is no other side.

Little Lollies of Sunshine

There isn't a word in English
or even an ancient language like Hebrew
to describe a parent when her child dies.

Would a *word* help my grief?
If anyone had told me she's in a better place,
I'd have punched them.

I'm not hungry. I am hungry.
What am I hungry for? *Kuchi sabishii*—
the mouth feels lonely and needs to chew.

In the eighth century they wrote
Requiescat in pace on gravestones,
May the person who died rest in peace.

Now we say R.I.P. Why
do we give flowers when someone dies?
Are *thoughts and prayers* supposed to comfort us?

There's a Romanian word. *Dor.*
Like Roar. Or floor. Or Labrador.
It means to long for someone you love.

It doesn't quench my longing—
I still feel like an orphan.

So sorry for your loss, they say.
Do they mean loss or lost?

Perhaps I don't need a word—
I could tell the bees.

In Medieval Europe people believed
bees were holy, a link between

humans and the spirit world,
part of the family. When someone died,

the *goodwife* had to go to the hive to tell the bees
of the loss to prevent further tragedies.

> *Little bees, our beautiful Mahalia is dead.*
> *Please stay with us in our distress.*

I can't tell the bees—I don't have a hive,
but I know the importance of bees
goes beyond superstition, that "colony collapse

disorder" is causing the deaths of billions
of bees. And without them,
oranges, almonds, avocados, and coffee

would disappear. Forever. Honey too.
Stop spraying your lawns
with chemicals.

When lawns became a symbol of wealth,
dandelions became a sign of neglect,
of poverty, and we called them weeds.

Let the dandelions be.
Bees and butterflies love them.
So did Mahalia. As an herbalist

she knew *Dent-de-lions*
to be full of vitamins and minerals—
and called her clinic *Dandelion Naturopathic*.

Anyone anywhere in the world
can identify the yellow lollies.
Next time you blow a puffball to make a wish

remember they are flowers
that welcome the bees, and the butterflies,
and think of Mahalia, our dandelion crusader.

Cushion Creeper

Fifteen years ago my friend
Diane went to a fancy event
at the Huntington Museum—
with food & wine & famous people
like Mickey Rooney, Michael York,
& that 101-year-old woman
from the Titanic.
Someone passed gas,
during a quiet moment,
but no one laughed.
They were a posh crowd.

I don't know how or why
Diane's email popped up
in my inbox today,
& though it wasn't funny,
I couldn't stop laughing,
& lay on the carpet,
tears running down my cheeks.
My husband
thought I'd hurt myself.
After I told him,
Someone farted at the Huntington,
he replied, *All this hilarity*
& hysteria because of a fart
fifteen years ago?

Anytime I'd giggle
like a *nincompoop*
Mahalia knew
it was about a fart,
& she'd laugh with me,
because she understood
it was a stupid habit

I learned from my mother,
who always giggled & blushed,
& called it *cushion creeper*
if we heard her toots.

Thinking of them I stopped laughing.
Because they're both dead—
my mother and my daughter.

Samsara

Hold the sadness and pain of samsara in your heart.
Then the warrior can make a proper cup of tea.
—Chogyam Trungpa

You died. It took me a while to understand
I hadn't caused your cancer. We all die.
We all live with grief. They say I'll laugh
again one day. My friend Anne
committed suicide at Niagara Falls, her kids
same ages as mine. A picture taken two decades

ago at Niagara Falls, my parents with my uncle
visiting from Israel. Religious, he drank his tea
Middle Eastern style in a glass with lemon.
For the Sabbath—Shabbat Shalom—
my mother had to keep the bathroom light
on for twenty-four hours. You always left

two or three cups of tea around the house
and we daren't throw those sips away. Rooibos,
with rice milk. What a fuss when our religious

niece visited us. We had to cover a shelf
in the fridge with paper towels for her kosher
ready-roast-chicken. Age eight, you silently
watched as she ate her special food on paper
plates with plastic cutlery. Not wanting to waste
we had her leftovers the next day—*But Mummy,*
you said, *It tastes of chicken.* The F.D.A.

warns two ounces of black licorice daily
for two weeks can cause heart rhythm problems.
It's my favorite candy. Am I eating too much?
I know you don't treat family, but you're a doctor.
I still have the licorice *caplets* you gave me—

For energy, you said.

Where are you?   Please call.

I found a postcard you sent us with a picture of a loon:
paddling in a small lake
we came upon a moose munching things,
stopping to watch her we heard loons
and the wind in the silence,
while the bugs feasted on us.

I know those silent buggy Ontario lakes.
Why didn't I know
I'd need to remember your laughter?

The Three Questions

When your dad and I emigrated from South Africa
in the olden days before the internet,
and cell phones in our pockets,
long distance calls were an expensive treat.
Our parents always shouted
the same three questions—

How are you?

How's the weather?
The cold and snow in Canada
scared our family in Jo'burg.

What can we send you?
Dried fruit? Rooibos tea? Biltong?

and always ended,
We love you. We miss you.

That was the call.

I'd give anything to hear your
Hi Mumsy,
and ask you the three questions—
How are you?
Is it warm over there?
Where are you? I have your rooibos tea.

"If We Could Dream Back Everything We Lost"

after Ellen Bass

"It's Mama's birthday today.
She would be forty-four,"
you tell your grandchildren
on a FaceTime call.

"But she died," says Isaiah
age four.

"Yes, she died, and we all miss her,
but we can still remember
her birthday," you say.

"Who will make the cake?"
he asks.

My Wet Eyes Stared Into Their Lights

During our family FaceTime call
at Chanukah last year,
we lit the fifth-day candles
on the menorah,
and my seven-year-old granddaughter,
the image of her late mother,
asked us,

> *Who misses Mama the most?*

I've spent the whole year wondering
how to answer.

At a Shabbat dinner on Friday night
when the woman opposite me said,
Where are your children?
I could tell her my son lives in Canada.
But I don't know where my daughter
is—she didn't leave a forwarding address
when she left.

Only a Green Thing

The tree which moves some to tears of joy,
is in the eyes of others only a green thing
—William Blake

Nemophilist, an ancient Greek word
for a *haunter of the woods,*
is a perfect way to describe

Mahalia. Instead of weeping
for her, I'm going to dry my eyes,
and take her two children hiking.

I'll teach them everything I know.
Everything she taught me.
She knew about *shinrin-yoku*

long before the rest of us rushed
out for our forest-baths. She knew trees
were sacred givers of life and keepers

of wisdom. On every walk in the woods
she'd greet the plants and trees,
asking them for guidance and healing.

Gingko leaves are fan-shaped,
Bodhi leaves look like a heart,
Pacific Hawthorn heals cancer.

It's thanks to her I am friends with
chamomile, yarrow, and dandelion.
She taught me to ask permission

of a plant before picking, to never pick
the entire crop—leave half for next
year—and to always say *thank you,*

even when picking stinging nettles.

ABOUT

According to Jewish tradition everyone dies twice. The first time
when they stop breathing and the second when the dead person's
name is spoken, or thought of, for the last time. I hope this little book
of poems will prevent Mahalia from dying a second time.

There's so much I can tell you about Mahalia. She was a born healer
and great listener. She qualified as a naturopathic doctor and
followed her calling with a passion. She loved to hike, camp and
canoe in the Ontario wilderness, always seeking, finding and
admiring the healing properties of wild plants and nature, in the
company of her closest friends. She was happily married to Erin and
pregnant with their second child when they moved with their two-
year-old daughter to Vancouver where Mahalia found tranquility
near the old trees and ocean.

A colonoscopy four months after her baby was born revealed that
Mahalia had Stage 4 cancer.

ACKNOWLEDGMENTS

My sincere thanks to the editors of the following journals in which these poems, or earlier versions of them appeared:

Blue Heron Review: "Little Lollies of Sunshine"
Contrary Magazine: "How Deep in the Valley" (nominated for the Best of the Net)
Literary Mama: "If We Could Dream Back Everything Lost"
MacQueen's Quinterly: "Only a Green Thing" (as "The tree which moves some to tears of joy, is in the eyes of others only a green thing,"), "This Isn't About You," "A Fearful Thing," "Your Name is a Poem"
ONE ART: "A Poem Begins With a Lump in the Throat," "The Stranger," "My Wet Eyes Stared into their Lights"
Storyteller Poetry Review: "Our Time Together, Too Short," "Samsara"
Silver Birch Press: *One Good Memory Series*: "Sleepless"
Verse-Virtual: "The Hardest Part," "Signs," "Little Lollies of Sunshine," "Only a Green Thing," and "How Deep in the Valley"
Writing in a Woman's Voice: "Nine Months," "A Week After She Left Us"

Many people helped me grow as a poet. I am grateful to you all, and give special thanks to a few:

Diane Chung, who helped me find the courage to take the leap.

Dinah Berland, the godmother of this book.

Sheri Johnson, who got me to write a poem a day in April 2020 only five weeks after Mahalia died. Many of these poems were written during that period of intense grief.

The participants of Eric Morago's *Your Poem, Your Voice* and Dinah Berland's *Poetry Oasis* workshops for their nourishing feedback and encouragement.

Women who Submit for a submission grant.

Donna Hilbert, Dinah Berland, and Jim Lewis who wrote supportive and insightful blurbs for my book.

Shannon Phillips of Picture Show Press for producing this beautiful chapbook for Mahalia.

Endless gratitude to my husband Reuben and our son Jeremy.

More Poetry Books from Picture Show Press

A sip of wind by Nora Simões
Alinea by Betsy Mars
Along the Fault Line by Tamara Madison
Between the Spine: A Collection of Erotic Love Poems
by Adrian Ernesto Cepeda
Concrete's Song by Lloyd David Aquino
daughter of salt by Chestina Craig
Girl On The Highway by Wendy Rainey
If your body is a broken landscape by Kathryn McMurray
Little Threats by Suzanne Allen
Quiver: A Sexploration by Holly Pelesky
Suddenly, All Hell Broke Loose!!! by Brian Harman
The Feather Ladder by Cindy Rinne
Witness: Selected Poems by George Hammons

www.ingramcontent.com/pod-product-compliance
Lightning Source LLC
Chambersburg PA
CBHW021147020426
42331CB00005B/938